APR 2017

T5-CNZ-388

DISCARD
FCPL discards materials that are outdated and in poor condition. In order to make room for current, in-demand materials, underused materials are offered for public sale.

BIG WAVE SURFING

Diane Bailey

Rourke Educational Media

rourkeeducationalmedia.com

Scan for Related Titles and Teacher Resources

Before & After Reading Activities

Level: M **Word Count: 3,422 Words**
100th word: *the* page 4

Before Reading:

Building Academic Vocabulary and Background Knowledge

Before reading a book, it is important to tap into what your child or students already know about the topic. This will help them develop their vocabulary, increase their reading comprehension, and make connections across the curriculum.

1. Look at the cover of the book. What will this book be about?
2. What do you already know about the topic?
3. Let's study the Table of Contents. What will you learn about in the book's chapters?
4. What would you like to learn about this topic? Do you think you might learn about it from this book? Why or why not?
5. Use a reading journal to write about your knowledge of this topic. Record what you already know about the topic and what you hope to learn about the topic.
6. Read the book.
7. In your reading journal, record what you learned about the topic and your response to the book.
8. After reading the book complete the activities below.

Content Area Vocabulary
Read the list. What do these words mean?

carve
confirm
cutback
duck dive
fins
gun
oceanographers
personal watercraft
rail
rip current
set
stamina

After Reading:

Comprehension and Extension Activity

After reading the book, work on the following questions with your child or students in order to check their level of reading comprehension and content mastery.

1. What materials were original surfboards made of? What are they made of today? Why the change? (Summarize)
2. Surfers wear safety gear suited for the water. When you are in the water, what kind of gear do you need? (Text to self connection)
3. Why is it important for surfers to study the ocean? (Asking questions)
4. What is a duck dive and why is it important? (Summarize)
5. Why do surfers need to be in great shape? (Infer)

Extension Activity
After reading about big wave surfing, think about how you could express the excitement and dangers a surfer feels by writing a short story. Make sure your story has a beginning, middle, and end. Use adjectives to describe your surfer and the setting. Share your story with your family, teacher, or classmates.

TABLE OF CONTENTS

JAWS! 4

GETTING STARTED 6

SPORTS SKILLS 14

GEAR UP 26

THE STARS 34

THE RIDE OF A LIFETIME 42

GLOSSARY 46

INDEX 47

SHOW WHAT YOU KNOW 47

WEBSITES TO VISIT 47

ABOUT THE AUTHOR 48

JAWS!

Shane Dorian was in Hawaii, on the North Shore of the island of Maui. The waves here are well-known to surfers. They are big and fast. Surfers call them "Jaws." Shane had been surfing for hours. It was getting late and the sun was going down. It was almost time to call it a day. Shane decided to look for a small wave and head in. Then he looked out to the horizon. A giant **set** of waves was coming in. He saw them stacking up, building speed. They were about a minute away. The jaws were opening.

The second wave of the set looked perfect. The wall of water was smooth, and it was moving fast. Shane decided to go for it. He started paddling out and stood up on his board. His knees were bent and his arms out. His surfboard was just a speck of red on the blue ocean. Shane was nervous. Was he in the right spot to catch the wave? Or would the ocean win this time?

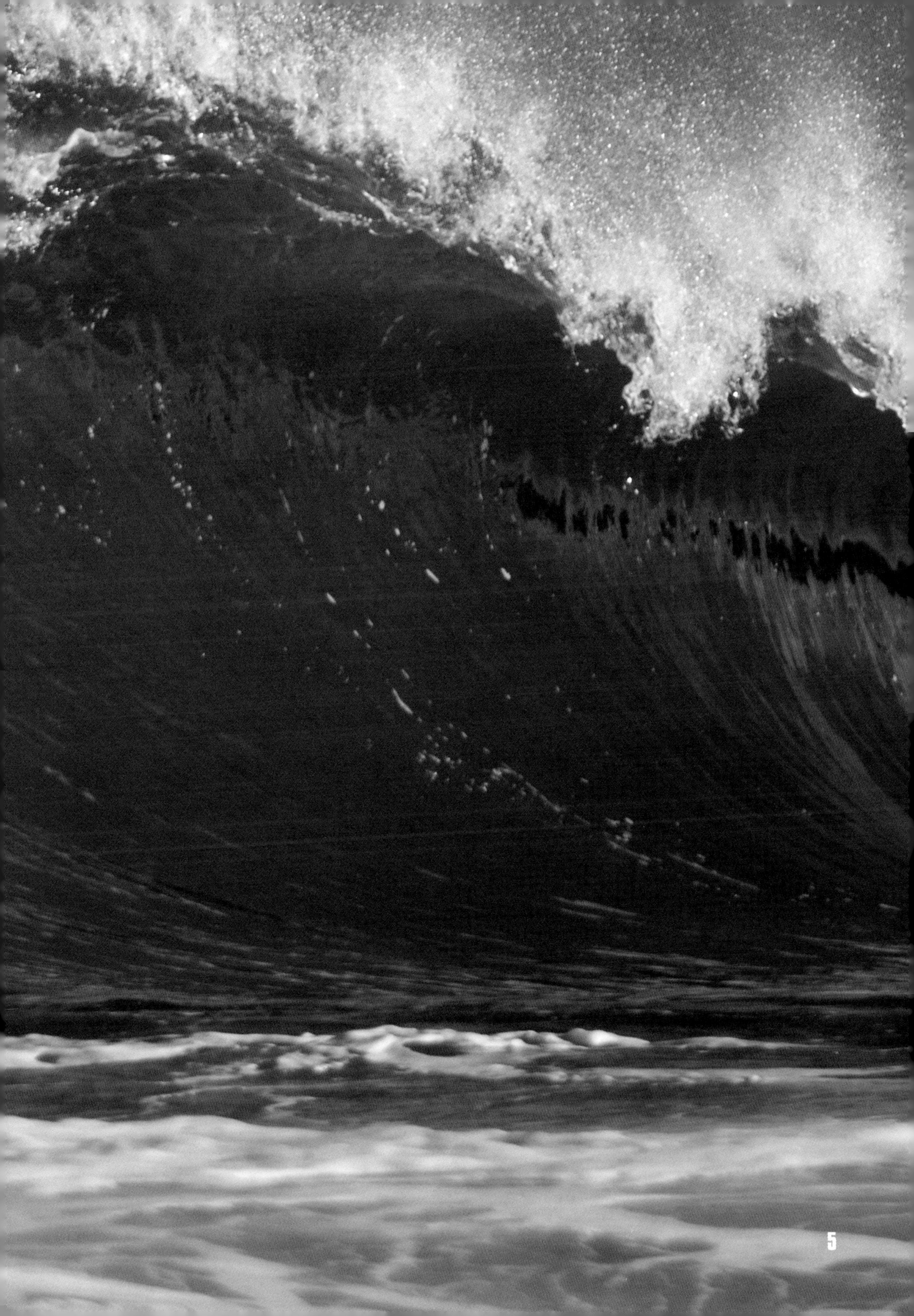

GETTING STARTED

Eddie Would Go

Eddie Aikau (1946–1978) was a big wave surfer from Hawaii who won many surfing competitions. He died in a boating accident in 1978. Afterward, a surfing contest called "The Eddie" was named for him. Modern surfers challenge each other to tackle big waves. They say, "Eddie would go."

Head to the beach on a sunny day and you will see surfers hitting the waves. In many places, the waves are only knee high. That is perfect for some watery fun on a hot afternoon, but it's not enough for big wave surfers. These athletes want bigger waves—much bigger. They look for waves that are 25 to 30 feet (7.6 to 9.1 meters) tall. Sometimes surfers catch waves that are even taller. These waves mean more than a longer, faster ride. Ocean waves are incredibly powerful. More height means more danger, and requires more skill.

Big wave surfers conquer waves that can be a big as buildings!

Surfing has been around for thousands of years. It started on islands in the South Pacific Ocean. Kings from ancient Hawaii surfed to show their skill and power. In the early 1900s, a famous American writer named Jack London

Surfers on average-size waves slice across the surface of the water.

visited Hawaii. He wrote an article about the surfing culture. A lot of people read his article. They started to become interested in the sport, too.

By the 1930s, surfers began to explore new beaches in Hawaii where the waves got higher. One of these was the beach of Makaha, on the island of Oahu. Another was on the island's North Shore. The North Shore was dangerous. Some surfers died when trapped in the waves. Only the bravest surfers dared to try it.

Duke's Wild Ride

Duke Kahanamoku was a famous Hawaiian swimmer and surfer. In 1917, he paddled into some waves that were about 30 feet (9.1 meters) high. He rode one for almost two miles (3.2 kilometers).

Duke Kahanamoku (1890–1968)

This 1953 photo inspired surfers to challenge the big waves of Hawaii.

In 1953, a photographer took a picture of three surfers riding a 15 foot (4.5 meter) wave. The picture caused a sensation. Big wave surfing was about to get even bigger. Surfers came to Hawaii and camped out on Oahu's North Shore. They ate fish and coconuts, and waited for the waves. In 1957, Greg Noll became the first surfer to try the dangerous waters of Waimea Bay in Hawaii. There, the swells could reach 20 feet (6 meters) or more.

Surfing got more popular during the 1950s and 1960s. It became a cultural phenomenon. Movies, television shows, and music all featured surfing. People from California to Australia to South Africa were trying it.

Better Boards

As surfers got better, so did their gear. The first surfboards were made of wood. They were hard and heavy. By the 1950s, people started to make surfboards out of foam and other lightweight materials. They added fins to keep them more stable and help in steering.

Garrett McNamara is one of the most successful big wave surfers around.

For some surfers, a 20 foot (6 meter) wave is small! They ride the monsters. Garrett McNamara holds the world record for the biggest wave ever surfed. In 2011, Garrett was towed by a **personal watercraft** far off the coast of Portugal. Then he rode in on a wave that was 78

> It's difficult to figure out just how tall an ocean wave is. You can't take a tape measure out there! Instead, experts study photographs and videos of the waves. That helps them determine how high they are.

feet (23.7 meters) high! Later, Garrett rode another huge wave in the same spot. It was estimated to be about 100 feet (30.4 meters) tall. Surfers Carlos Burle and Andrew Cotton also rode waves that were probably that high. However, it was not possible to **confirm** the heights of their waves, so Garrett still holds the record.

In 2012, Shawn Dollar set another impressive record. He did not use a personal watercraft to get to the wave. Instead, he paddled out on his own at Cortes Bank, off the coast of California. There, he caught a 61 foot (18.6 meter) wave.

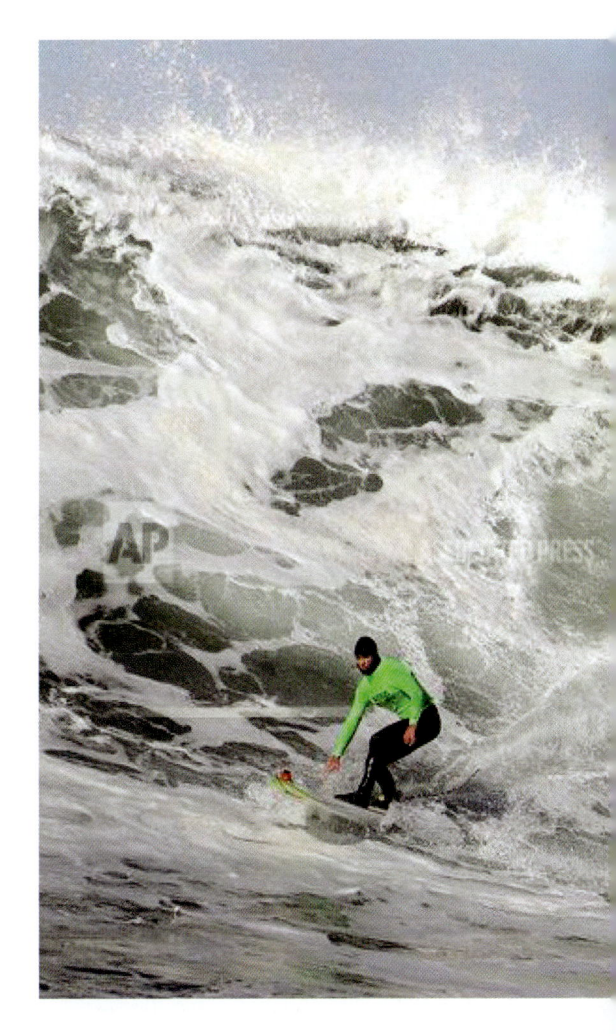

Shawn Dollar wraps up a ride on another big wave.

SPORTS SKILLS

Big wave surfers are sort of like **oceanographers**. Before they ever get their feet wet, they spend time watching the waves. How tall are the waves? What is the distance between them? How often do they come in? No two waves are exactly the same, but by watching closely, surfers can get an idea of the general pattern. This way they know what they are up against. In the water, they identify the highest point of the wave they plan to ride. Then they determine which side of the wave is steeper. This shows the direction the wave is traveling. Surfers position themselves near the top of the wave and travel down the steep slope.

Surfers have to learn how to study the ocean as they wait for just the right wave to ride.

Surfers have to balance carefully on their boards, even as they speed along.

Before you can ride the waves, you have to get to them, usually by paddling.

It's great to ride a wave in, but first surfers have to get out there. That is hard work. The whole power of the ocean is pushing the waves in. Surfers need strength, **stamina**, and skill to paddle against them. Surfers lie on their stomachs on the board. They keep their legs out of the water so they do not drag and slow them down. They cup their hands, fingers together, to push as much water back as possible with each stroke. Bigger waves start farther from shore. That means more paddling. Sometimes surfers can find a **rip current**, which helps move them out. Rip currents can be extremely powerful and dangerous. Surfers must practice to use them safely and not get sucked down.

The Surfer's Workout

One of the basic skills for a surfer is being a good swimmer. They must also work to stay fit. They lift weights to build their arm muscles. Running and other workouts develop stamina. It helps if they can hold their breath a long time, too!

Ducking under a thundering wave lets it pass right over you.

Waves look a lot bigger in the water than they do from the shore. It can be scary to watch a huge wave moving in. Surfers have ways to let waves pass over them without getting slammed. One method is the **duck dive**. To do this, they push the nose of the board underneath the wave. Then they use their feet and the weight of their bodies to help push the rest down. They duck their head under the water as the wave passes over them. Then they shift their weight to the back of the board to bring it back level.

The duck dive is more difficult in big waves. It is important to time it just right. If a surfer dives too late, the wave will catch him and toss him around. If he dives too soon, he will come up before the wave has gotten past.

Here's an underwater view of a surfer going under a wave.

19

A surfer takes off on a ride, starting at the top of the wave.

Eventually, all that paddling pays off. It is time to ride back in. Catching a wave depends on good timing. Surfers point the nose of the board toward the shore. As the wave approaches, they paddle as hard as they can. They want to gain speed and momentum. This helps them get on top of the wave so it can carry them forward.

After catching the wave, surfers need to pop up, or stand. They lie on the board with their head and shoulders raised slightly. Their hands grip the board. Then, in one move, they jump into a standing position. They stand sideways, with their feet pointed to the long edge of the board. Experienced surfers practice until they can pop up quickly and smoothly.

Which foot forward?

If someone pushes you from behind, which foot do you use to step forward and stop the fall? That is probably the foot that will feel most comfortable at the front of the board. Most surfers ride with their left foot forward. A surfer who puts their right foot forward is called a "goofy-foot."

Now, ride the wave! Surfers learn to use the power of the wave to move through it. Turns start with the hands and shoulders. Surfers point their bodies where they want to go and then rotate their hips into the turn. Then they shift the weight of their feet to follow the direction of the turn. One way of turning is to **carve** through the water. Surfers push the **rail**, or edge of the board, into the water to steer the board into large turns.

To turn, surfers lean their bodies in the direction they want to go.

Surfers also want to stay near the top of the wave, just under the lip. This is where most of the power is. If they get pushed out of this zone, they can do a **cutback**. This is a fast, zig-zag turn. The surfer angles the nose of the board back to the top of the wave, and then quickly swings the tail around to follow. This puts the surfer back into a good position.

Surfers can make sharper turns by pushing the nose of the board around with their legs.

Up, up, and then down! A surfer flies off his board for a watery landing.

Even the best surfers mess up sometimes. They do not catch a wave just right, or they lose their balance. Then they wipe out in a 20 foot (6 meter) wall of water! Wiping out is never fun, but there are good ways to do it if necessary. If possible, surfers want to be in the barrel of the wave, so they come out the back. They avoid the lip of the wave. When it breaks, it feels like falling onto the ground. They try to lead the fall with their backside. It does not look graceful, but it helps protect their head.

Now what do they do? Relax! There is no way one person can battle the ocean. The best thing to do is to take a deep breath, hold it, and stay calm. Panicking uses up more oxygen. They wait for the wave to pass, and then surface before the next one hits.

When a surfer is knocked off the board, it is called a wipeout.

GEAR UP

Expert surfers own a lot of different boards. All together, they are called a quiver. Surfers choose which one to use depending on the surf conditions. At a glance, the boards look flat. A closer look shows they have slight curves at the ends and on the bottom. These help them grip the water.

Big wave surfers often use a surfboard called a **gun**. These surfboards are narrow and long, sometimes 12 or 13 feet (3.7 to 4 meters). They are pointed at both ends.

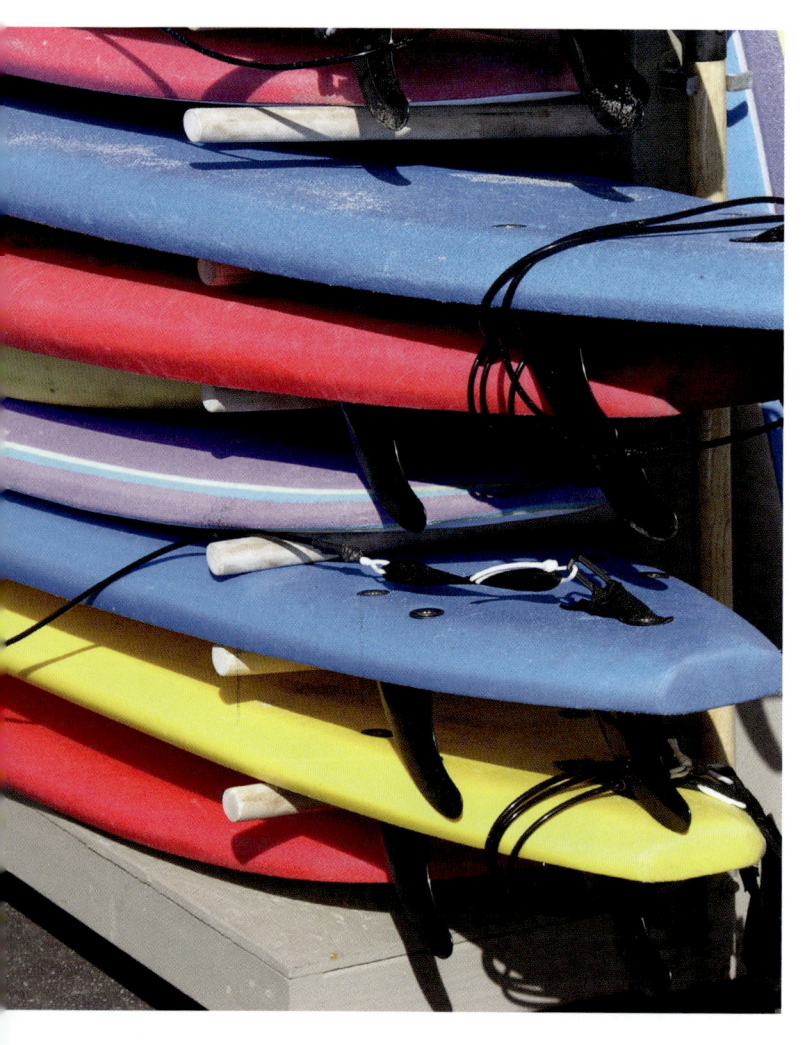

Surfboards come in a wide variety of sizes, shapes, and colors.

Surfers must work hard to paddle into big waves. They must go fast to overcome the wave washing against them. A longer board helps them gain more speed. The long rail helps them control the board once they are on a wave.

Surfboard Shapers

People who make surfboards are called shapers. They might use wood, foam, fiberglass, or other materials. They can add details to the board that match a surfer's personal style. They also make boards that are suited to specific surfing locations.

Fins on the bottom rear of surfboards help the surfer steer the board.

Many surfboards come with **fins** mounted near the tail. They look like shark fins, but they are on the bottom, not the top! The fins push against the water in a sideways motion. This keeps the board more stable. They also let the surfer steer and control the board by shifting his weight from side to side.

You can't surf if you are not on the board! Surfers have great balance, but they also use several tools to help keep them in place. First, they apply a coat of wax to the surfboard. The wax forms small bumps on the smooth surface of the board. It gives the surfer's feet something to grip. Some surfers also use traction pads. These are textured pads that stick to the surface of the board.

A flexible rubber leash keeps the surfboard from floating away after a wipeout.

Many surfers tie their boards to their legs with a leash. If they wipe out, the surfboard will float. They can follow the leash back to the board.

Go Green

It can be difficult to find a surfer in the middle of the ocean. Some surfers carry dye packs. They spill bright green dye into the water to help rescuers find them. The dye is safe for sea life and fades after about an hour.

A 30 foot (9.1 meter) wave can push a surfer far underwater. Many surfers wear a special paddle vest. It is not as bulky as a regular life vest, so the surfer can still lie on the board and paddle. Other surfers wear wetsuits that can inflate if necessary.

The wetsuit has an empty pouch sewn on to the back. It also has a can of carbon dioxide. Carbon dioxide is a type of gas that can be squeezed into a small space.

In an emergency, the surfer pulls a cord

Before a surfer hits the big waves, he makes sure his inflatable vest is working.

that fills the pouch with the carbon dioxide.
It blows up into a small balloon and helps
lift the surfer to the surface.

Waves farther out in the ocean are taller and move faster. Surfers who paddle out can usually only go out far enough to get 20 to 25 foot (6 to 7.6 meter) waves. As big wave surfing caught on, some surfers wanted to get even bigger waves. That required a whole new type of gear. In the 1990s,

Using personal watercraft has changed how big wave surfers reach the waves.

some surfers began using personal watercraft to tow each other farther out into the ocean. Some surfers even use helicopters to pull them out to the big waves.

Tow-in surfing is a team sport. Besides the surfer, there is at least one other person who operates the personal watercraft. Backup members of the team ride on other boats or watercraft. Surfing such huge waves is incredibly risky. The team is ready to help in case the surfer gets into trouble. They get a rescue board to the surfer, who is then towed out of the danger zone as fast as possible.

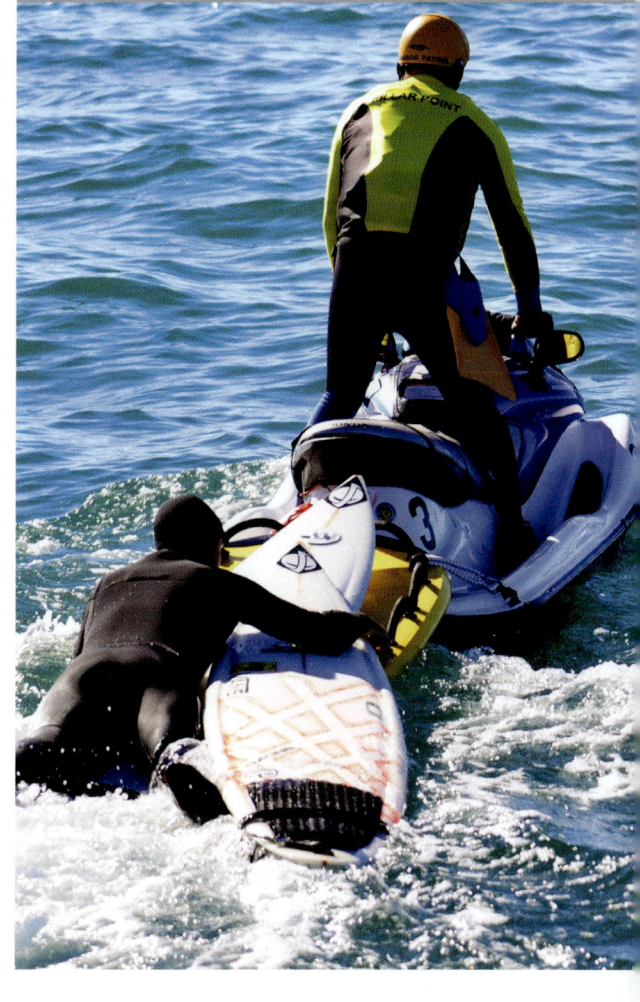

A ride home after a long day in the waves is a welcome sight for a big wave surfer.

THE STARS

Big wave surfing is just one of the adventurous sports Laird Hamilton takes on.

Surfers are not fearless—they are too smart for that. Instead, they are brave even in the face of danger. Many of big wave surfing's biggest stars have faced death and survived. Take a look at some of the sport's best athletes:

LAIRD HAMILTON

Laird Hamilton got an early start with being in the water. He grew up in Hawaii, and his dad was also a surfer. Laird was a risk-taker as a child. One time he was out with his dad. As soon as his dad wasn't looking, he jumped off a high cliff into the water! Laird has won many surfing competitions and surfed waves that are almost 80 feet (24 meters) high. He helped develop tow-in surfing, so he can go farther out to catch even bigger waves. He also likes other extreme sports such as snowboarding, skydiving, and motocross. When he is not in the water looking for a challenge, he makes films and television shows about extreme sports.

Laird plunges down a wave in Tahiti in the South Pacific.

GREG LONG

Greg Long grew up in Southern California, where his father was a lifeguard. Greg learned about the ocean before he even learned to walk. He started surfing when he was 10, and began competing at age 12. Since then, he has won several important surfing contests. Greg takes surfing seriously. He studies waves to learn how to surf them. He was in a bad accident in 2012 and almost died. His knowledge of the ocean helped him overcome his fear. He went back out again just a few weeks later.

Greg Long, left, shows off his championship big wave riding form.

Keala Kennelly also rides smaller waves in pro surfing events.

KEALA KENNELLY

Most big wave surfers are men. Keala Kennelly is one of the women who stands out. She was raised in Hawaii and both of her parents were surfers. Keala started surfing at age 5 and turned professional at age 17. In 2010, she won the first women's big wave competition in Oregon. She has also won prizes for being the year's best female surfer in 2011, 2013, and 2014. Keala has wiped out and gotten injured, but she always comes back for more. She proves that women can be big wave surfers, too.

Surfers wait impatiently for the news that the big waves are back at Mavericks.

Starting in January each year, surfers know the message can come at any time: the Titans of Mavericks contest is on. This event is one of the most important in big wave surfing. Mavericks is located near San Francisco, California. The coast there receives giant waves that sometimes reach 60 feet (18.2 meters). Organizers of the event watch the surf closely to determine when it will be biggest. Then, they invite 24 of the world's best surfers to come. They have only 24 hours to get there. It is an honor to win the contest, but it is more important just to get out there. Surfers all want the same thing: to ride the big waves.

Just Jeff

Jeff Clark grew up near Mavericks. He saw the monster waves, but he did not see any surfers out there. In 1975, when he was a teenager, he decided to tackle them. Jeff could not get anyone to go with him. For 15 years, he was the only surfer at Mavericks. Finally, word spread and other surfers began to take on the dangerous Mavericks waves.

Big waves are kind of like the surfers who ride them. They all have their own personalities. Surfers like different places based on their own styles. Waimea Bay in Hawaii has large and often dangerous waves. It was one of the first places for big wave surfing, and is still a favorite. Another challenging place in Hawaii is "Jaws," off the island of Maui.

Other huge waves can be found off the coast of Portugal in Europe. They can reach almost 100 feet (30.4 meters) tall. The records for the biggest waves ever ridden were set here. Cortes Bank is located about 100 miles

Big waves in Hawaii draw big crowds.

(160 kilometers) off the coast of California. Surfers must tow in to get to these powerful waves. The waves form next to an island that is completely underwater. Australia, South Africa, and Tahiti are other popular places.

Surfing star Garrett McNamara rides the whitewater off Portugal.

THE RIDE OF A LIFETIME

Shane Dorian caught the wave at Jaws. He sped down, the water hitting his face. The wave was perfect: giant and gnarly, but with a clean face. Shane thought it would be easy after all. Then, about halfway down the wave, he saw something. A big bubble of water churned in the wave, coming up from the reef below. There was no way around it. He had to go over it.

Shane took a wider stance on his board and braced himself.

Shane Dorian learned his surfing skills on smaller waves before tackling the giants.

As the wave pitched him forward, his board slowed down. It was like he was going over a speed bump in the water, but there was no stopping now! Shane nearly fell, but he made it over. Success! Caught up in the moment, he stretched his arms out in triumph. Then he realized his ride was not over. In fact, he wasn't even halfway through.

Shane surfs on another massive wave.

When a wave starts to break, it can form a tube.

Shane was in the barrel of the wave, and it was still in charge. Quickly, he brought his arms back in. He still had to survive his ride. In front of him, he saw the wave changing shape. Water rushed up the face of the wave. The spray spat at him, just past his head. The power was amazing.

Time seemed to slow down. Shane had always hoped to catch a perfect wave like this. Now, he had to use all his skills and experience to ride it correctly.

Nearby, people on jet skis and boats watched. Shane disappeared in the spray, deep in the barrel. When he came back out, everyone yelled and cheered. Shane rushed down the face of the wave and reached the end. Totally pumped up, he pounded the water with his fists. He'd done it! He completed the ride of a lifetime.

For his awesome ride, Dorian earned an award for "Ride of the Year."

GLOSSARY

carve (KARV): to make a long, smooth turn with a surfboard

confirm (kuhn-FIRM): to make sure something is true or accurate

cutback (KUT-bak): a quick, zig-zag move to reposition the surfboard

duck dive (DUK DIVE): a way of passing underneath a wave

fins (FINZ): small steering attachments on the bottom of a surfboard

gun (GUN): a long and narrow surfboard good for big wave surfing

oceanographers (oh-shun-AHG-rah-fers): people who study the science of the ocean, including waves and currents

personal watercraft (PER-sun-uhl WAHT-er-kraft): a small, motorized vehicle for the water, often used by just one person

rail (RALE): the long edge of a surfboard

rip current (RIP KERR-ent): a strong, narrow current located close to the coast

set (SET): a group of waves

stamina (STAM-ih-nah): the ability to do something for a long time

INDEX

Aikau, Eddie 6
Clark, Jeff 39
Cortes Bank 40
Dollar, Shawn 13
Dorian, Shane 4, 42, 43, 44
fins 28
"Jaws" 4, 40
Hamilton, Laird 34, 35
Kahanamoku, Duke 9
Kennelly, Keala 37
Long, Greg 36
McNamara, Garrett 12, 13
Noll, Greg 11
North Shore 4, 9, 11
safety 30, 31
surfboard shapers 26, 27
Titans of Mavericks 38, 39
tow-in surfing 32, 33
Waimea Bay 40

SHOW WHAT YOU KNOW

1. Where was the record set for the biggest wave ever ridden?
2. What are two things a surfer looks for when watching waves?
3. How do fins on a surfboard help a surfer?
4. What are the characteristics of a gun surfboard?
5. Why do some surfers like tow-in surfing?

WEBSITES TO VISIT

www.clubofthewaves.com/surf-culture/big-wave-surfers.php

www.thesurfchannel.com

www.surfscience.com

ABOUT THE AUTHOR

Diane Bailey has written about 40 nonfiction books for kids and teens, on topics ranging from science to sports to celebrities. She also works as a freelance editor, helping authors who write novels for children and young adults. Diane has two sons and two dogs, and lives in Kansas.

Meet The Author!
www.meetREMauthors.com

© 2016 Rourke Educational Media

All rights reserved. No part of this book may be reproduced or utilized in any form or by any means, electronic or mechanical including photocopying, recording, or by any information storage and retrieval system without permission in writing from the publisher.

www.rourkeeducationalmedia.com

PHOTO CREDITS: Cover © TKTKTKT; AP/Wide World: Francesco Seco 10, 13, 42. Dollar Photo: Francesco Marra 14; Janet Wall 16; Monkey Business Images 17; Stefan Schur 18; Trubavink 19; Gkphotoart2012 21; Geoff Tydeman 22; Dod 27; Patrick Stedrak 28. Dreamstime: Manaphoto 7, 36, 42; Nihon Japan 8; Pikappa 9; Funniefarm5 11; Gmf1000i 12, 32; Nalukai 15; ChrisVanLennepPhoto 20; MDA 23; Kazsano 24; Tinalau 25; Alancroswaithe 26; GeoffGoldSwain 29; Paparico 34; Nalukai 38, 40, 43; Epicstockphoto 44. Mercator Media: 30. Newscom: Terry Schmitt/UPI. John Salanoa: 31. Shutterstock: Brian A. Witkin 33; EpicStockMedia 35; Manaphoto 37.

Edited by: Keli Sipperley
Produced by Shoreline Publishing Group
Design by: Bill Madrid, Madrid Design

Library of Congress PCN Data

Big Wave Surfing / Diane Bailey
(Intense Sports)
ISBN 978-1-63430-438-2 (hard cover)
ISBN 978-1-63430-538-9 (soft cover)
ISBN 978-1-63430-626-3 (e-Book)
Library of Congress Control Number: 2015932641

Printed in the United States of America, North Mankato, Minnesota

Also Available as:
ROURKE'S e-Books